First published in the United States of America in 2018 by Chronicle Books LLC.
Originally published in Australia in 2016 under the title *Lots* by Penguin Random House.

Library of Congress Cataloging-in-Publication Data available.

ISBN 978-1-4521-6514-1

Manufactured in China.

Design and handlettering by Marc Martin.
The illustrations in this book were rendered in watercolor, gouache, pencil, and digital collage.

10 9 8 7 6 5 4 3 2 1

Chronicle books and gifts are available at special quantity discounts to corporations, professional associations, literacy programs, and other organizations. For details and discount information, please contact our premiums department at corporatesales@chroniclebooks.com or at 1-800-759-0190.

Chronicle Books LLC
680 Second Street
San Francisco, California 94107

Chronicle Books—we see things differently. Become part of our community at www.chroniclekids.com.

EVERYTHING & EVERYWHERE

A FACT-FILLED ADVENTURE FOR CURIOUS GLOBE-TROTTERS

by Marc Martin

chronicle books · san francisco

YOU ARE HERE

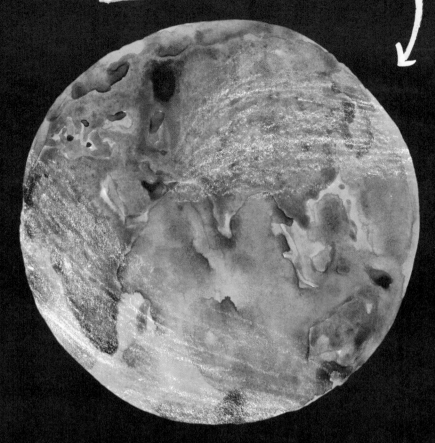

...or maybe you're here?

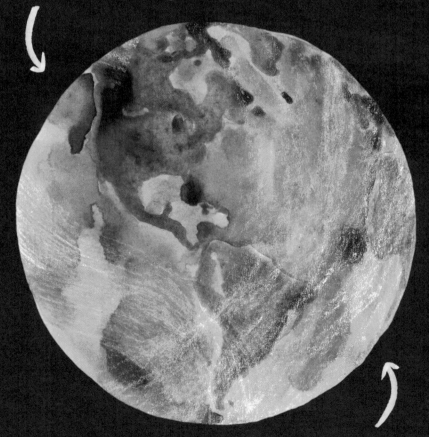

Maybe one day you'll go here.

A NOTE FROM THE AUTHOR

How many cats live in Cairo? How many languages are spoken in New York? What is pylsusinnep? These are just some of the many questions you might ask about the world we live in.

The following pages are a gathering of facts, thoughts, and observations about our planet as seen through the eyes of an artist. Some may intrigue you, some may surprise you, and some may leave you with more questions than answers.

From cities to forests and from deserts to oceans, there's so much to discover. All you need is a good guide and a little curiosity...

So what are you waiting for? Let's start exploring!

ANTARCTICA

The coldest and windiest continent on Earth. Bring a good jacket!

Southern right whale

WHALES
Feed in the nutrient-rich Southern Ocean

Minke whale

Human size compared to whale size

Finback whale

Sperm whale

Blue whale
Weighs 420,000 pounds

Killer whale (orca)

Humpback whale

PENGUINS
20 million breeding pairs of penguins

Adélie penguin

ATM
One place to get money on the whole continent (McMurdo Station)

Gentoo penguin

Emperor penguin

Chinstrap penguin

ROSS ICE SHELF ← 500 miles across →

ICEBERGS
Of all shapes and sizes

SOME OF THE RESEARCH STATIONS
From all around the world

Bharati Station (India)

SANAE IV (South Africa)

Princess Elisabeth Station (Belgium)

Neumayer Station III (Germany)

Jang Bogo Station (South Korea)

Taishan Station (China)

Halley VI Station   (United Kingdom)

Amundsen-Scott Station (United States)

Concordia Station (France/Italy)

ICEBREAKERS
Used to clear a path for other boats

SNOW PETRELS
Breed exclusively in Antarctica

SHIPPING CONTAINERS
Used to transport supplies

WIND
Up to 200 miles/hour

BLUE SKIES
As far as the eye can see

ROAD TRAINS
Long trucks with many trailers

WINDMILLS
For pumping water

ROAD TRAINS
53 METRES LONG

← Long straight roads →

DINGOES
The largest terrestrial predators in Australia

BUDGERIGARS
Fly in large flocks, and are very noisy!

MAJOR MITCHELL'S COCKATOO

OPAL
Found in the mining town of Coober Pedy

Bad hair day

COOBER PEDY

ROAD WARNING SIGNS ARE FOR YOUR PROTECTION PLEASE DON'T USE THEM FOR TARGETS

ROAD SIGNS
For every occasion

NEXT 96 km

GALAHS
Also known as rose-breasted cockatoos

The Australian Aboriginal Flag

HONG KONG

An island city in China with bustling streets and crowded skylines, and it's one of the world's most densely populated metropolises

MARKETS AND SHOPPING

Sneakers street

Computer market

Jade market

Costume market

Goldfish market

Flower market

FRAGRANT HARBOR
"Hong Kong" translates to "Fragrant harbor" in Chinese!

Business-card market

FERRIES
135,000 passengers a day going to more than 260 outlying islands

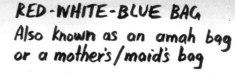

A SYMPHONY OF LIGHTS
The world's largest permanent light and sound show

RED-WHITE-BLUE BAG
Also known as an amah bag or a mother's/maid's bag

SIGNS
Everywhere!

AIR CONDITIONERS
So humid in summer!

Duddell Street
Hong Kong's
only gas lamps

**STAIRS AND
ESCALATORS**
For all those hills

Ladder
Street

20 minutes
from top to
bottom

Central–Mid–Levels
escalator (the longest
outdoor escalator
in the world)

DOUBLE-DECKER TRAMS
The world's largest fleet of
double-decker trams

**EXPENSIVE
CARS**
More Rolls-Royces
per person than in
any other city

DIM SUM

Bite-sized portions of food, such as

- Beef tripe
- Chicken buns
- Pork buns
- Custard buns
- Chicken claws
- Custard roll
  sponge cake
- Pork and shrimp
  bean curd roll

BUBBLE TEA
Frothy tea
mixed with
tapioca balls

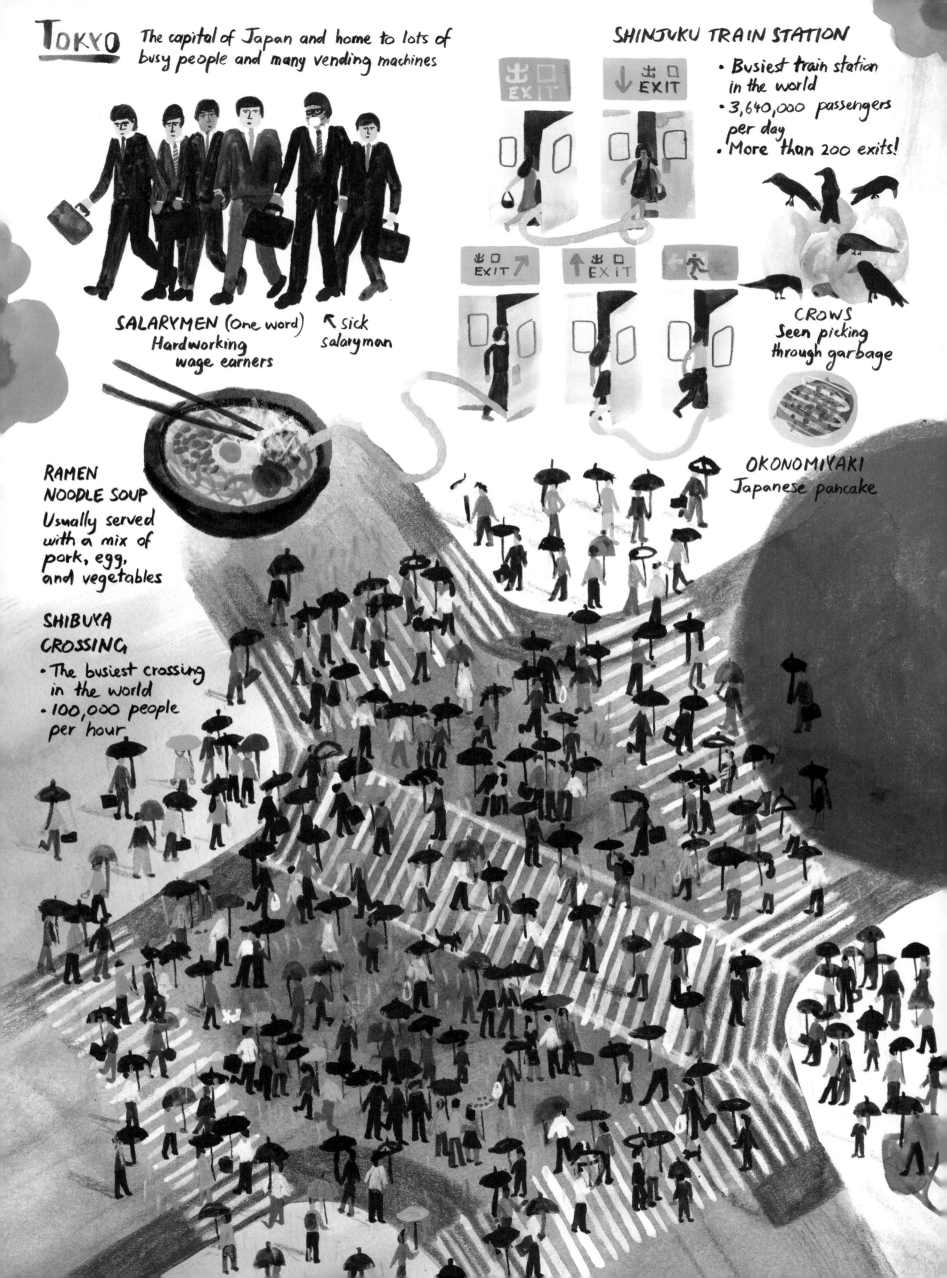

TOKYO
The capital of Japan and home to lots of busy people and many vending machines

SHINJUKU TRAIN STATION
- Busiest train station in the world
- 3,640,000 passengers per day
- More than 200 exits!

EXIT · EXIT · EXIT · EXIT · EXIT

SALARYMEN (One word)
Hardworking wage earners

↖ sick salaryman

CROWS
Seen picking through garbage

RAMEN NOODLE SOUP
Usually served with a mix of pork, egg, and vegetables

OKONOMIYAKI
Japanese pancake

SHIBUYA CROSSING
- The busiest crossing in the world
- 100,000 people per hour

VENDING MACHINES 5.6 million vending machines in Japan!

EXIT

Flowers · Umbrellas · Books · Beer · Ramen · Fish bait · Tap beer · Wrong exit! · Soft drink · Beer

Bananas · Beer · Underwear · Neckties · Milk · Coffee · More beer · Salad · Eggs

ONSEN
Japanese bathhouse

SHINKANSEN FAST TRAIN
Travels at 200 miles/hour

GODZILLA
Official citizen of Japan and has very bad breath

Sushi train

KAWAII
Cute things

Cute toast
Cute potato
Cute cat
Cute cloud
Cute rice

CONVENIENCE STORES
On nearly every corner

EXIT

Lobster vending machine

CHERRY BLOSSOMS
Enjoy hanami (flower viewing) in March/April

CICADAS
The sound of summer in Tokyo

ULAANBAATAR

The capital of Mongolia—one of the least densely populated countries in the world

GENGHIS KHAN (c.1162–1227)
aka Chinggis Khaan
Emperor of the Mongol Empire and featured on anything and everything

Genghis Khan drinks

Genghis Khan Equestrian Statue

130 feet high

Genghis Khan money

Genghis Khan stamps

Genghis Khan hotel

CHINGGIS KHAAN

Genghis Khan airport

MONGOLIAN FOOD

Süütei tsai
Salty tea

Airag
Fermented mare's milk

Guriltai Shul
Noodle soup

Aaruul
Dried milk curd

Buuz
steamed mutton dumplings

Khuushuur
Deep-fried dumplings

GERS
Portable round tents where many Mongolians live

NAADAM
A traditional festival consisting of wrestling, archery, and horse racing

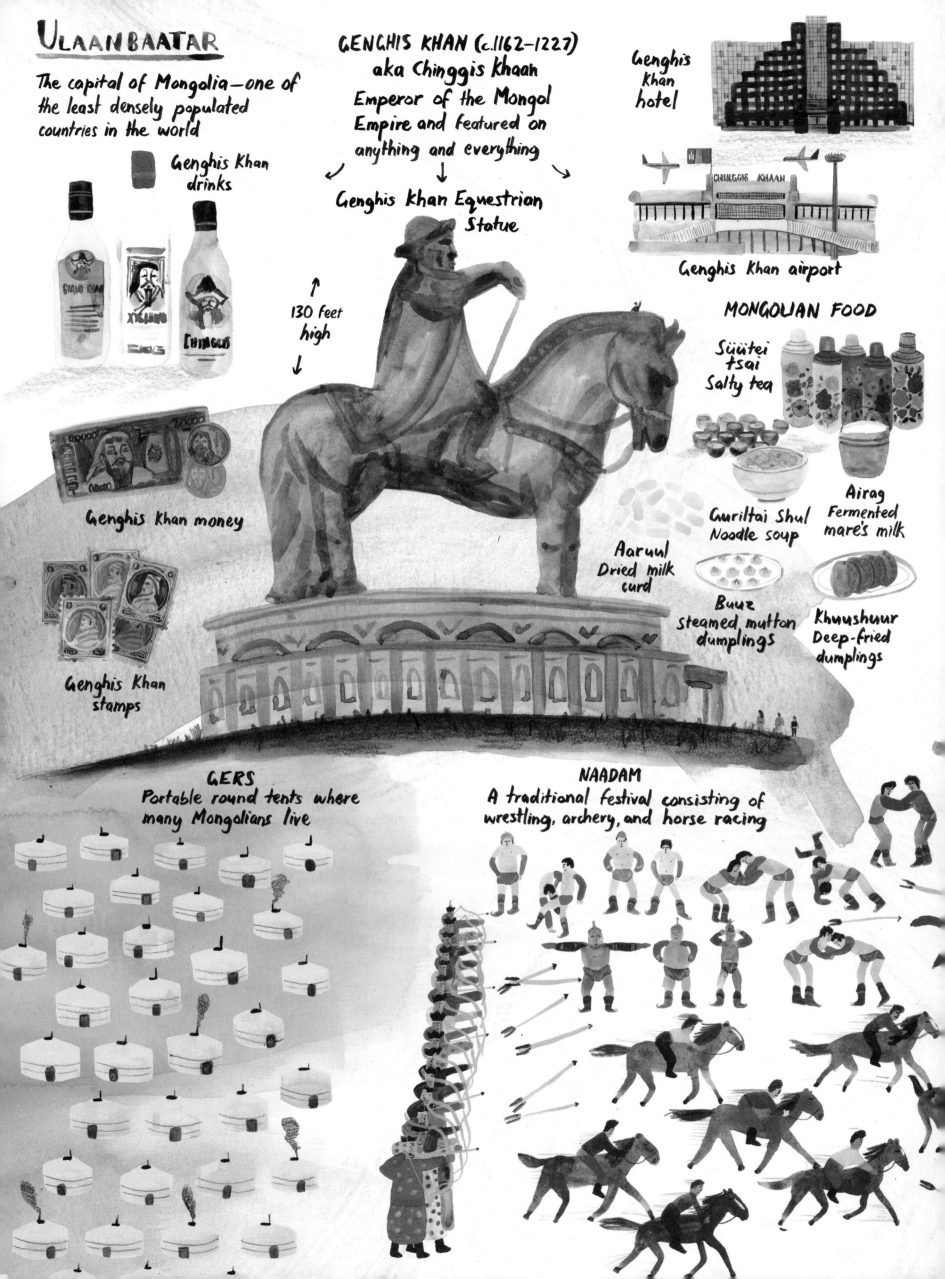

← FURGON VAN
Officially seats nine, but usually fits as many as possible

BACTRIAN CAMELS
Two humps!

OVOOS
Sacred cairns made from rocks and wood. Circle three times clockwise for a safer journey while traveling.

YAKS
Used for their thick, shaggy fur and very tasty milk

MONGOLIAN HORSE
Short, stocky breed, native to Mongolia

GOBI DESERT
Approximately 500,000 square miles and Asia's largest desert

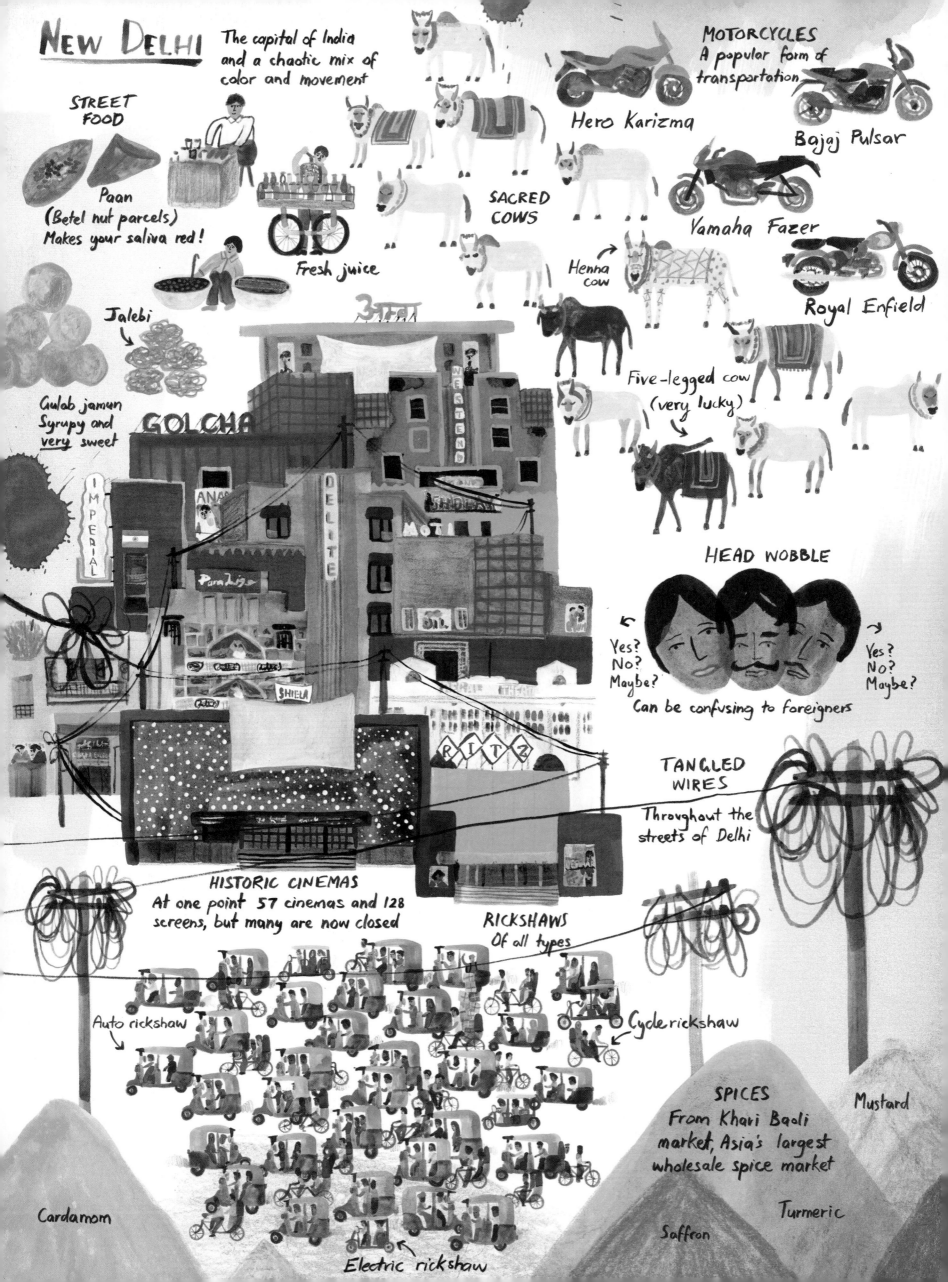

MANY MUSTACHES
In all shapes and lengths

BUSES
World's largest fleet of environmentally friendly gas-powered buses

BANGLES In many colors

CHAI WALLAHS
Make a great cup of tea

HENNA
Used for decoration in ceremonies and special events

WEDDINGS
Especially during wedding season
(Roughly Sept-Feb)

DEITIES
A small selection...

Lakshmi

Ganesha

Vishnu

Parvati

Saraswati

Brahma

CHILI FOR MOTHER-IN-LAW (HOT!)

Shiva

CHAI CUPS
Made of clay.
Break after drinking

Cumin

Fennel

Chili

Nutmeg

Moscow

The capital of Russia, where babushkas, billionaires, and borscht collide

COLD
-14°F in winter

Borscht stain
↳ Whoops!

STALIN'S SKYSCRAPERS
Also known as The Seven Sisters

Moscow State University

Kotelnicheskaya Embankment Building

Ministry of Foreign Affairs

BILLIONAIRES
Roughly 80 billionaires in Moscow

CATHEDRALS AND CHURCHES
that look like candy

Saint Basil's Cathedral

The Cathedral of Saint Michael the Archangel

MONUMENTS

Georgy Zhukov
← Famous military officer

Laika the dog
(the first animal to orbit the Earth)

← Monument to the Conquerors of Space

Vladimir Lenin →

Member of The Beatles

Communist revolutionary, politician, and theorist

The Church of the Holy Trinity

Church of the Intercession

Peter the Great
May have named himself →

Alexander Pushkin →
Poet, playwright, and novelist

Worker and kolkhoz Woman

Malchik monument
A famous stray dog that lived in the metro

Leningradskaya Hotel

Hotel Ukraina

Kudrinskaya Square Building

Red Gates Administrative Building

MATRYOSHKA DOLLS
A traditional Russian toy
(not to scale!)

POLICE OFFICERS
Around 50,000 of them

STRAY DOGS
An estimated 35,000 stray dogs, with some
known to ride the trains for food

PARK POBEDY METRO
The longest escalators
in Europe

413 feet high
740 steps

← Yuri Gagarin
Cosmonaut and
the first human
in outer space

METRO
STATIONS
Palatial and
practical!

Kiyevskaya

Mayakovskaya

Elektrozavodskaya

Taganskaya

Komsomolskaya

9 million passengers per day

CAIRO

The largest city in the Middle East, the capital of Egypt, and a great place to make a feline friend

TAXIS
Lots of black-and-white taxis and lots of honking horns

TRAFFIC
More than 4.5 million cars

CATS
Found on every street corner, empty seat, and sidewalk in the city

bella

DOORKEEPERS (BAWABS)
They mind the building, run errands for tenants, and find parking spots!

455 feet high

GREAT PYRAMIDS OF GIZA

Pyramid of Menkaure

Queens' Pyramids

Pyramid of Khafre

Pyramid of Khufu
Approximately 2.3 million stone blocks

KHAN EL-KHALILI BAZAAR
A major shopping district for antiques, jewelry, and general goods

GOLD, BRASS, AND SILVER GOODS

Plates

Jugs

Lamps

Bowls

EGYPTIAN FOOD

Fesikh
Fermented, salted, and dried gray mullet

Fül Medames
Cooked fava beans with oil, cumin, and parsley

Duqqa
A mixture of herbs, nuts, and spices

Kushari
A mix of rice, macaroni, and lentils

Mulukhiya
A soup made from finely chopped leaves from the jute plant

Gibna Domiati
A soft, salty cheese typically made from buffalo milk

Shisha on the go!

SHISHA PIPES AND SHISHA SMOKERS
A smoking pipe for flavored tobacco, a very popular pastime

MINARETS
Cairo's nickname: "The city of a thousand minarets"

PARIS

The capital of France, rich in art, food, and culture

The Mona Lisa (difficult to see)

De l'art!

THE LOUVRE MUSEUM
- 650,000 square feet of galleries
- Employs 2,100 staff
- Has 8 million visitors a year

CHEESE
Best served at room temperature

Brie

Camembert

Maroilles

Chèvre

Beaufort

Laguiole

Roquefort

Valençay

Comté

DOGS
About 200,000 of them

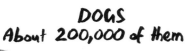

10 tons of dog droppings every day

Watch your step!

CAFE TABAC

LE SEBASTO

Café de Flore

CAFE DE FLORE

ROOFTOP APARTMENTS
Great views!

PLEIN SOLEIL

LE PURE CAFE

TERRACE BARS AND CAFÉS
Around 9,000 places to get a drink

PHARMACIE

PHARMACIES
For all your health
and beauty needs

Pharmacy signs
everywhere

WINE (VIN)
Common varieties:
- Bordeaux
- Champagne
- Pinot noir
- Chardonnay
- Chenin blanc
- Merlot
- Grenache
- Malbec

ARC DE TRIOMPHE
12 avenues radiating from the center

BOULANGERIE

BOULANGERIE

Boulangerie Pâtisserie

BOULANGERIE · PÂTISSERIE

BOULANGERIE

BAKERIES Approximately 1,800

**LE TOUR
DE FRANCE**
- Up to 198 cyclists
- Approximately 2,200 miles
- 21 days long
- Always ends in Paris

Croissant

Pain au chocolat

Chausson
aux pommes

Pain aux
raisins

You can never
have too many
baguettes

Éclair

Flan

Mille-Feuille

Religieuse

Macarons

Croissant aux
amandes

CAKES AND PASTRIES

Not a
cake

Tarte
aux fraise

Opéra

Reykjavík

The capital of Iceland and home to many natural wonders and strange sauces

NAMES
The most common names in Iceland are Jón and Anna

(Labels throughout the crowd of people: Jón, Anna, Jón, Jón, Anna, Anna, Jón, Jón, Anna, Jón, Jón, Anna, Jón, Anna, Jón, Anna, Anna, Jón, Anna, Anna, Jón, Jón, Jón, Anna, Anna, Anna, Anna, Anna, Jón, Björk, Jón, Jón, Anna, Jón, Jón, Anna, Jón, Anna, Jón, Anna, Jón)

The cairn formerly known as Jón

GEOTHERMAL POOLS
Very warm!

VOLCANOES
130 in Iceland

ARCTIC FOX
The only native mammal in Iceland

ATLANTIC PUFFINS
60% of the world's Atlantic puffins nest in Iceland

Baby puffin

ICELANDIC HORSE
Very photogenic

Anna

Jón

Jón

CAIRN
A pile of rocks used as a marker

CANS
Icelanders drink more cola per person than any other country

HOUSES
Many colorful rooftops ↘

SAUCE

PYLSUSINNEP
Mustard sauce

A sauce for everything!
- Hamborgarasósa
- Kokteilsósa
- Remoladi
- Pitusósa
- Grænmetissósa

SKYR
A yogurt/cheese-like food eaten for breakfast, as a snack, or as a sauce

ARCTIC TERNS
Travel 44,000 miles every year, the longest migration route of any animal

FISHING BOATS

RE 358
RE 377
RE 391
RE 311

LICORICE
A popular treat

NORTHERN LIGHTS ↑
A spectacular light show caused by particles from the sun hitting the Earth's atmosphere

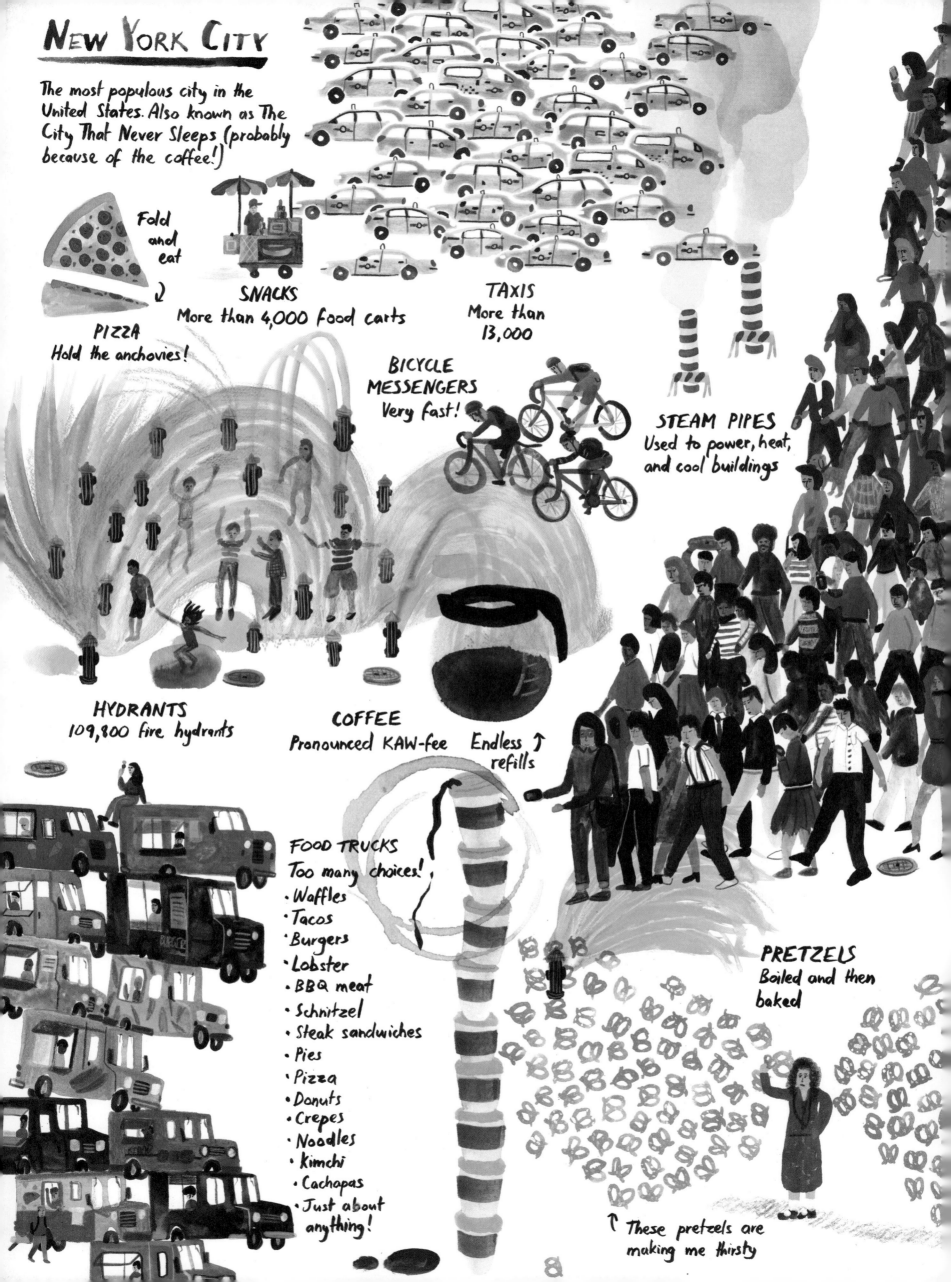

NEW YORK CITY

The most populous city in the United States. Also known as The City That Never Sleeps (probably because of the coffee!)

PIZZA
Hold the anchovies!
Fold and eat ↲

SNACKS
More than 4,000 food carts

TAXIS
More than 13,000

BICYCLE MESSENGERS
Very fast!

STEAM PIPES
Used to power, heat, and cool buildings

HYDRANTS
109,800 fire hydrants

COFFEE
Pronounced KAW-fee   Endless refills ↑

FOOD TRUCKS
Too many choices!
- Waffles
- Tacos
- Burgers
- Lobster
- BBQ meat
- Schnitzel
- Steak sandwiches
- Pies
- Pizza
- Donuts
- Crepes
- Noodles
- Kimchi
- Cachapas
- Just about anything!

PRETZELS
Boiled and then baked

↑ These pretzels are making me thirsty

RATS
Too many
to count!

TIMES
SQUARE
Many lights
and signs

Tower
of Bagels

Not only
used by men!

MANHOLE COVERS
264,000 manhole covers

PEOPLE
8.5 million people from all
around the world, speaking
more than 200 languages

CHRYSLER
BUILDING
3,862 windows in
the Chrysler Building

SKYSCRAPERS
Nearly 300
skyscrapers

BAGELS
Best served with
cream cheese

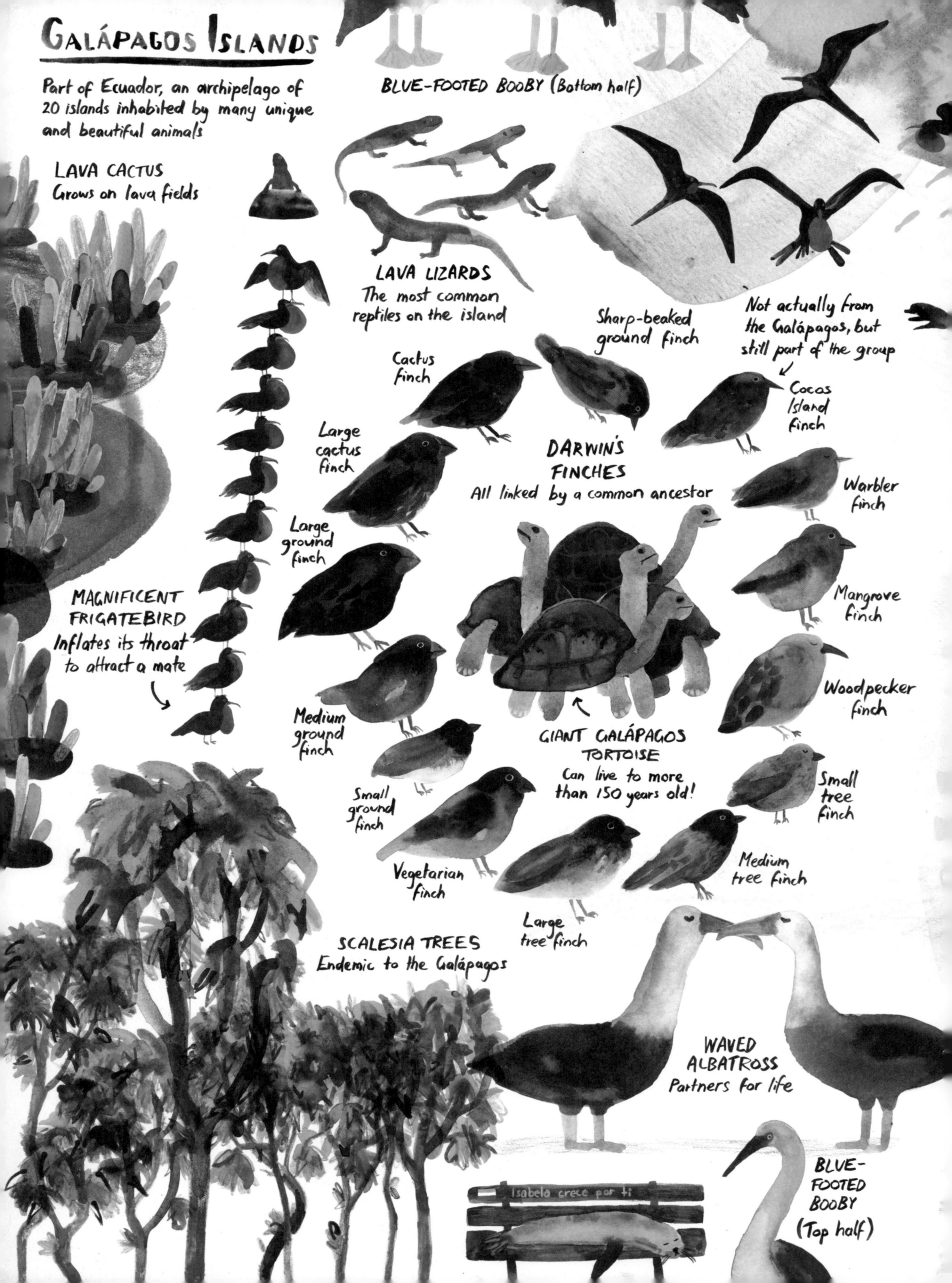

GALÁPAGOS ISLANDS

Part of Ecuador, an archipelago of 20 islands inhabited by many unique and beautiful animals

LAVA CACTUS
Grows on lava fields

BLUE-FOOTED BOOBY (Bottom half)

LAVA LIZARDS
The most common reptiles on the island

Sharp-beaked ground finch

Not actually from the Galápagos, but still part of the group
↓
Cocos Island finch

Cactus finch

DARWIN'S FINCHES
All linked by a common ancestor

Warbler finch

Large cactus finch

Large ground finch

Mangrove finch

MAGNIFICENT FRIGATEBIRD
Inflates its throat to attract a mate

Woodpecker finch

Medium ground finch

GIANT GALÁPAGOS TORTOISE
Can live to more than 150 years old!

Small tree finch

Small ground finch

Vegetarian finch

Medium tree finch

Large tree finch

SCALESIA TREES
Endemic to the Galápagos

WAVED ALBATROSS
Partners for life

Isabela crece por ti

BLUE-FOOTED BOOBY (Top half)

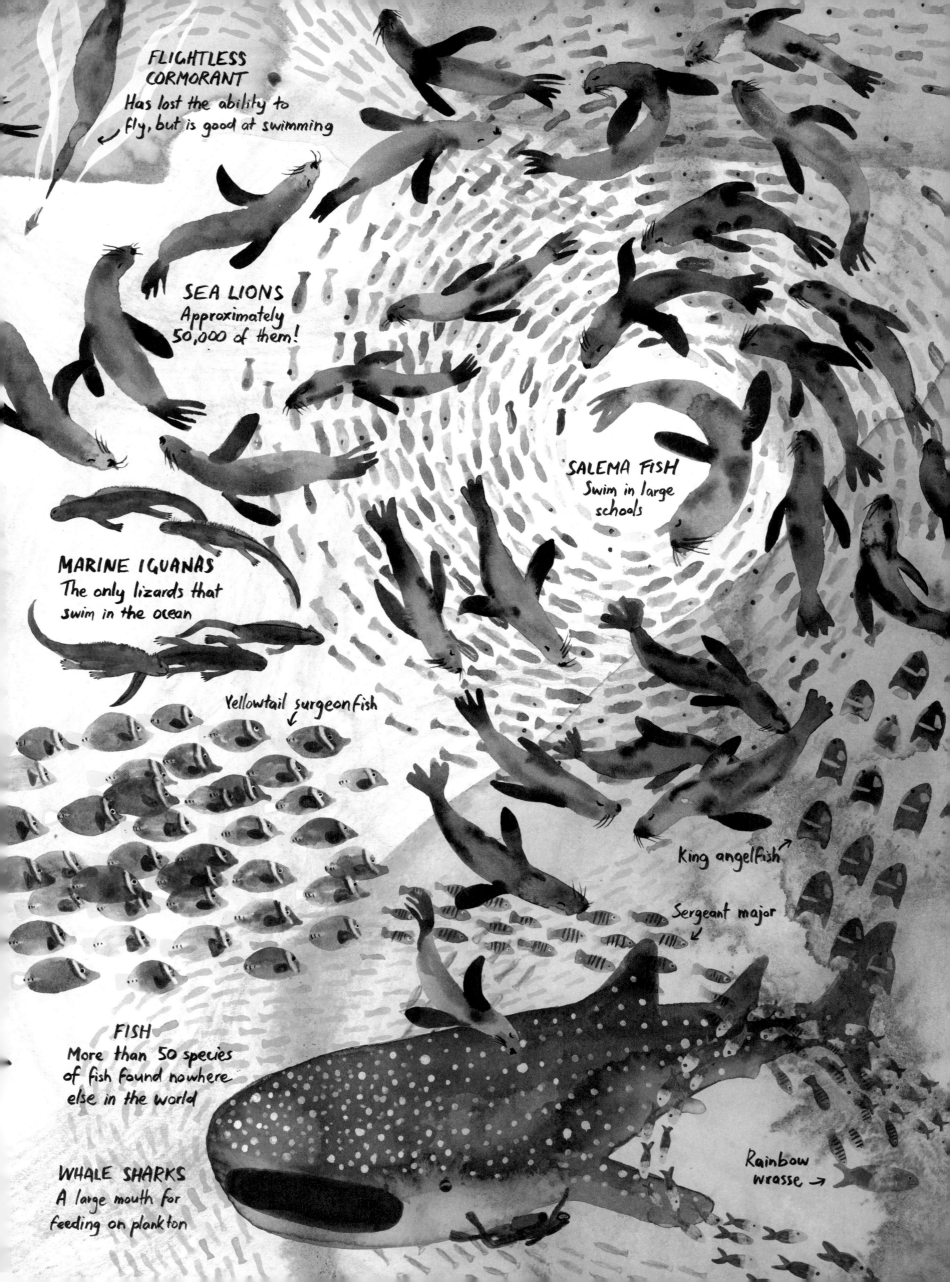

FLIGHTLESS CORMORANT
Has lost the ability to fly, but is good at swimming

SEA LIONS
Approximately 50,000 of them!

SALEMA FISH
Swim in large schools

MARINE IGUANAS
The only lizards that swim in the ocean

Yellowtail surgeonfish

King angelfish

Sergeant major

FISH
More than 50 species of fish found nowhere else in the world

Rainbow wrasse →

WHALE SHARKS
A large mouth for feeding on plankton

Amazon Rainforest

Traversing nine countries, the Amazon is the largest and most biodiverse area of tropical rainforest on the planet

FROGS
Glass frog
Blue poison dart frog
Poison dart frog
Surinam horned frog

BIRDS

Chestnut-fronted macaw
Spectacled owl
Amazon kingfisher
Blue-and-yellow macaw
Hyacinth macaw
Crimson topaz

SLOTHS
Very. Slow. Movers.

GREEN ANACONDA
Up to 20 feet long

Wire-tailed manakin

Scarlet macaw
Scale-crested pygmy tyrant
Grey-winged trumpeter
Swallow-tailed hummingbird

Oropendola
Plum-throated cotinga

Capped heron
King vulture
Blue-fronted amazon
Yellow-headed caracara
Masked trogon

CAPYBARAS
A large semi-aquatic rodent

AMAZON RIVER DOLPHINS
Also known as pink dolphins

RED-BELLIED PIRANHAS
Very sharp teeth!

BLACK CAIMANS

BASILISK LIZARD
(aka Jesus lizard)
Can walk on water!

ELECTRIC EELS
Shock their prey with 600 volts of electricity

TREES
16,000 different species of trees

KINKAJOU
Can turn its feet backward and run in the opposite direction

TOUCANS
Regulate body temperature with their beaks

MONKEYS

Spider monkey

Emperor tamarin

Capuchin monkey

Squirrel monkey

Marmoset

Rubber tree (Hevea brasiliensis)
Sap used to make rubber

Huasaí tree/palmito (Euterpe precatoria)

Barrigona, pona, or huacrapona (Iriartea deltoidea)

Palla, conta, or shapaja (Attalea butyracea)

Huicungo (Astrocaryum murumuru)

JAGUAR
The third-largest cat in the world

Walking palm/cashapona (Socratea exorrhiza)

Kapok tree (Ceiba pentandra)
Grows up to 230 feet high

ARAPAIMA
The Amazon's biggest fish

GIANT ANTEATERS
24-inch-long tongue

← Grows up to 10 feet →

GIANT OTTER

THE AMAZON RIVER
One of the longest rivers in the world

RIO DE JANEIRO

A city in Brazil surrounded by mountains and beaches, with a nonstop carnival atmosphere!

TIJUCA FOREST
The largest urban forest in the world ↓

SUGARLOAF MOUNTAIN
1,300 feet high

← **CHRIST THE REDEEMER STATUE**
100 feet tall and a lot bigger than this drawing

COATI
Lives in large social groups of up to 30 individuals

BOTECOS
A great place to enjoy a refreshing drink

Bar Bracarense

Boteco

BOTECO

BAR IO

BOTECO

Bar

RIO CARNIVAL
An annual festival filled with dancers, floats, and more than 200 samba schools

Don't forget your sunscreen! ↓

BEACHES
More than 30 miles of beautiful beaches

CAPOEIRA
A Brazilian martial art that combines dance, music, and acrobatics

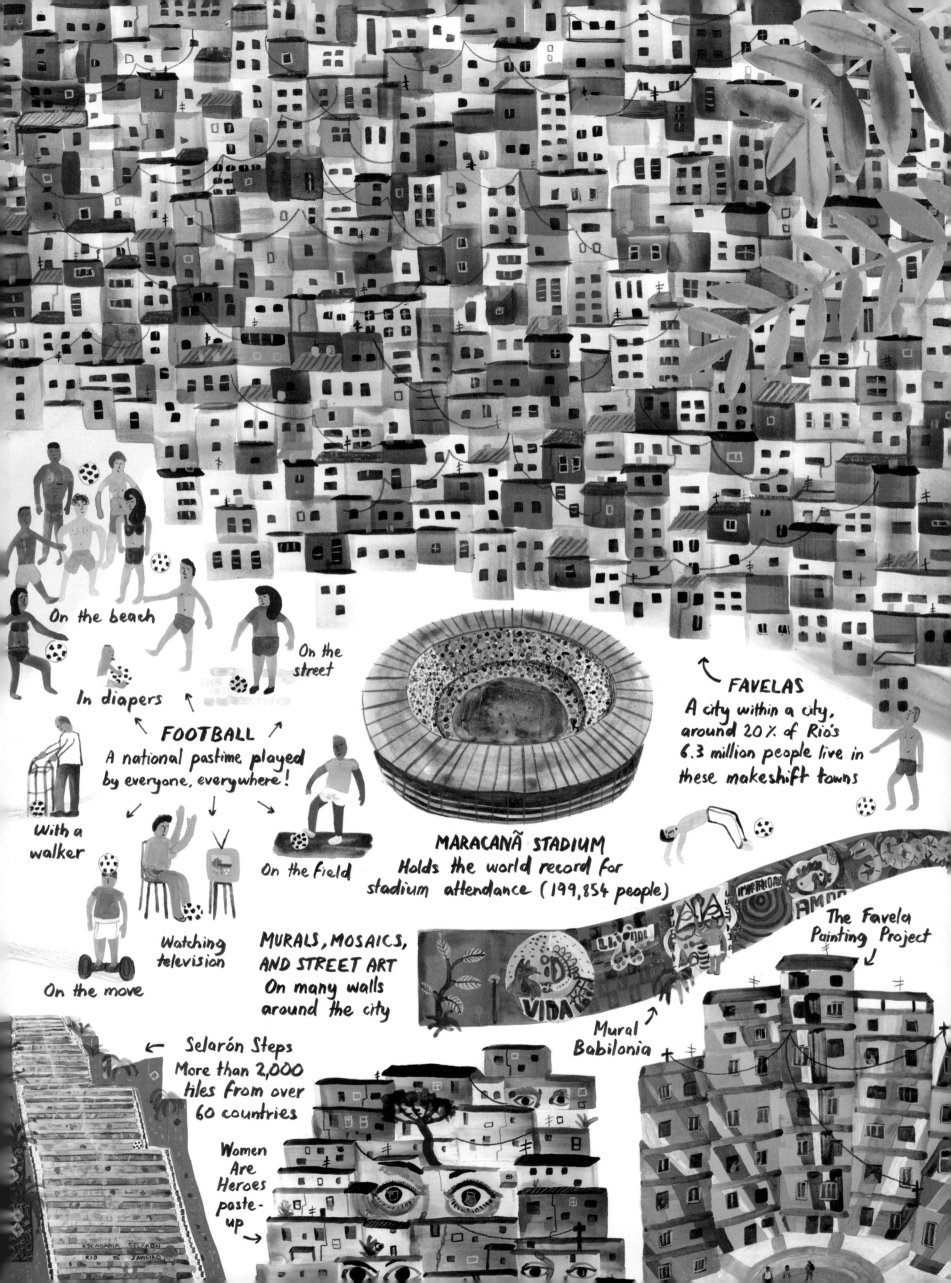

On the beach

On the
street

In diapers

FOOTBALL
A national pastime played
by everyone, everywhere!

With a
walker

Watching
television

On the field

On the move

MARACANÃ STADIUM
Holds the world record for
stadium attendance (199,854 people)

FAVELAS
A city within a city,
around 20% of Rio's
6.3 million people live in
these makeshift towns

MURALS, MOSAICS,
AND STREET ART
On many walls
around the city

The Favela
Painting Project

Mural
Babilonia

Selarón Steps
More than 2,000
tiles from over
60 countries

Women
Are
Heroes
paste-
up

CAPE TOWN

One of South Africa's three capital cities, a place of natural beauty with a diverse cultural history

TABLE MOUNTAIN
Approximately 600 million years old →

PORT OF CAPE TOWN
One of the busiest shipping corridors in the world

Get your swank on!

ARCHITECTURE
Influenced by Dutch, French, German, Victorian, and Malay styles

SWANKERS/SWENKAS
Well-dressed gentlemen competing to look the sharpest and swankiest!

Martin Melck House
One of the oldest colonial homes in South Africa

Houses of Parliament
Built in 1884

Bo-kaap ↑
Colorful homes built by Muslims from East Africa and South East Asia

Green Point Lighthouse
The oldest operational lighthouse in South Africa

Castle of Good Hope
The oldest building in South Africa
(built 1666-1679)

City Hall
Built in 1905

WHALES
Watch for migrating whales from July to November

BEACH CABINS
Colorful changing cabins (aka Umkleidekabine) at Muizenberg beach

BUTTERFLIES
Aeropetes tulbaghia aka
Table Mountain Beauty

ORCHIDS
Disa uniflora aka
The Pride of Table Mountain

CREATURES BIG AND SMALL

The Big Five
and
the Little Five

Lock your
windows!

African bush elephant

Cape elephant shrew

CHACMA BABOONS
Very intelligent and always
looking for an easy meal!

Rhinoceros

Rhinoceros beetle

Cape buffalo

Red-billed
buffalo weaver

Lion

Antlion

Leopard

Leopard tortoise

GREATER FLAMINGOS
Get their pink color from
pigments in the food they eat

SURFING
Lots of beaches,
lots of waves